The Japanese Giant Hornet

Kristin Cashore

Contents

What is the Japanese giant hornet?........................... 2

How do giant hornets work together? 4

How do giant hornets hunt?.. 8

How do honeybees fight giant hornets?...................10

How do giant hornets help? 12

How do giant hornets act around people? 14

Glossary 16

Rigby
A Harcourt Achieve Imprint

www.Rigby.com
1-800-531-5015

What is the Japanese giant hornet?

A **hornet** is a large insect, like a bee, with a very painful sting. The Japanese giant hornet is the biggest hornet in the world. The giant hornet lives in many Asian countries. It is most commonly found in the woodlands and mountains of Japan. The giant hornet is bigger than other hornets found around the world. Some grow to be 2 inches long!

JAPAN

Tokyo

Pacific Ocean

The Japanese giant hornet has a long stinger that quickly kills its food. However it does not hunt for other insects by itself. It always hunts with an army of giant hornets from its nest. They are mighty hunters, but they are also good protectors of their young and their nests.

How big is the Japanese giant hornet?

Japanese giant hornet, 2 inches

honeybee, 1/2 inch

How do giant hornets work together?

Giant hornets work together to take care of their hive. It's a big project.

First the hornet queen lays thousands of eggs. The eggs grow into young hornets called **larvae**. The larvae need a lot of food to grow. An army of adult hornets leaves the hive to hunt for food.

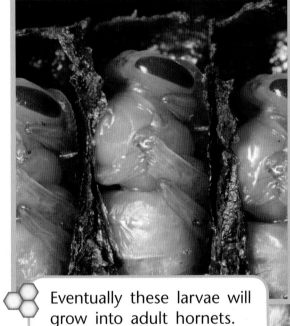

Eventually these larvae will grow into adult hornets.

The adult hornets kill insects like honeybees and other hornets. They bring the insects back to the hive to feed the larvae.

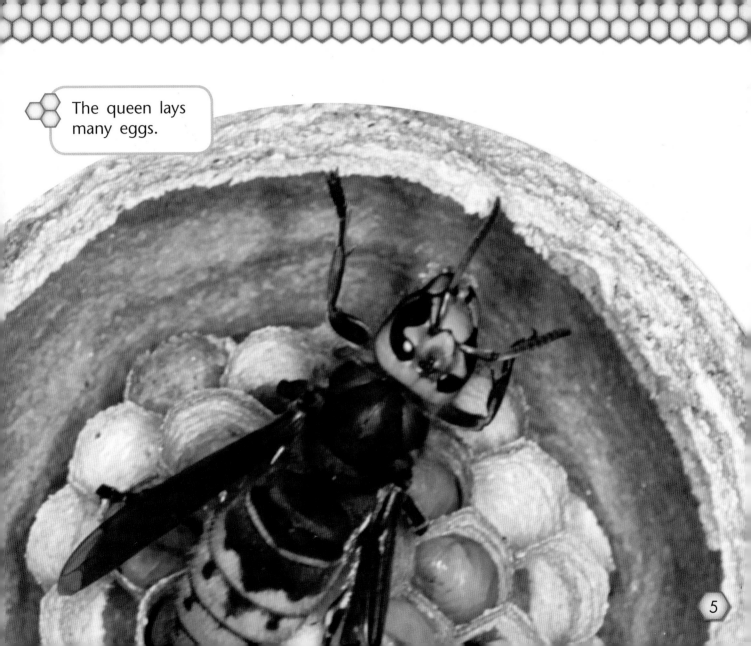

The queen lays many eggs.

5

The larvae cannot chew their own food. The adult hornets chew the food into a sticky paste and feed it to the larvae.

The adults and the larvae help each other.

The larvae thank the adults by paying them back. They pass a special liquid that contains a strong chemical to the adults. The chemical gives the adult hornets extra energy so that they can go hunt for more food.

How do giant hornets hunt?

Giant hornets hunt in groups. The European honeybee is one of their favorite foods. A single giant hornet can kill 40 honeybees in one minute. A group of giant hornets can destroy 30,000 honeybees in a few hours!

When a giant hornet finds a **colony** of bees, it marks the colony with a special smell. The smell quickly brings other giant hornets to the area. The hornets surround the bee colony on all sides and tear it apart. They carry the honeybee larvae back to their own hive.

group of giant hornets

Two or three giant hornets could destroy this honeybee hive in a few hours.

How do honeybees fight giant hornets?

Honeybees in Japan have shared the woodlands of Japan with these giant hornets for many years. Over time the honeybees have come up with a way to fight the hornets. They do it by working together.

When a hornet comes near their hive, about 500 honeybees attack the hornet. The bees crowd around the hornet in a tight ball. They beat their wings very fast and heat themselves up. The temperature inside the ring of honeybees rises to about 117 degrees Fahrenheit. That's hot enough to kill the hornet!

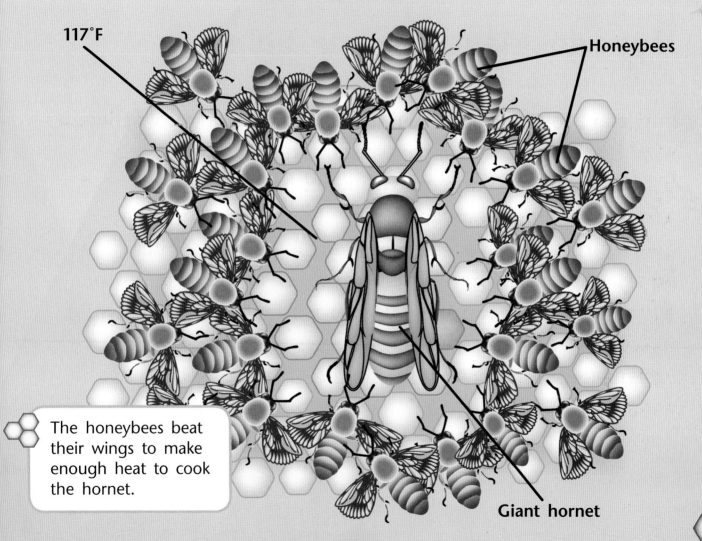

117°F

Honeybees

Giant hornet

The honeybees beat their wings to make enough heat to cook the hornet.

How do giant hornets help?

Giant hornets kill other insects, but they have an important job in Japan. Think of how many insects there would be in Japan if there weren't any giant hornets.

In Japan giant hornets live in the forest areas, but many Japanese forests are being chopped down. If the giant hornets have no place to live, they die. If there are fewer hornets, there are more honeybees. Having too many honeybees can be a dangerous problem for people in cities. The giant hornets do their part by helping to control the number of other insects.

Giant hornets kill honeybees, which helps keep the honeybee population down. But this beekeeper raises bees for their honey, so he keeps his bees safe from the giant hornets.

One kind of honeybee lives in a hive inside of a log.

How do giant hornets act around people?

Giant hornets usually don't sting people except to defend themselves or their hives. However, when they do sting people, it is very painful. The hornet sinks its long stinger into human skin. Strong **venom** pumps out of its stinger. This venom can burn through human flesh if the sting is not treated right away. About 40 people die every year in Japan after being stung by giant hornets. Hornets usually attack when people get too close to a hornet hive.

People should see a doctor right away if a Japanese giant hornet stings them.

In some parts of Japan, people eat giant hornets! Do you remember the energy liquid that the larvae give to the adult hornets during feeding? Today there is a sports drink that is based on the chemicals in hornet larvae. Some athletes feel they get an energy boost, thanks to the giant hornet.

Marathon winner Naoko Takahashi of Japan drinks a sports drink made from hornet larvae.

Glossary

colony a group of bees living together in a hive
hornet a large insect with a very painful sting
larvae young insects that have not yet grown into adults
venom poison